Buried Alive

poetry born of a life sentence

Roderick 'Rudy' Bankston

Also by Roderick 'Rudy' Bankston

Shed So Many Tears

Snippets of Soul in Seventeen Syllables

Order copies at **iAmWeClassics.com**

dedication

Donna and Pat. i continue to live in gratitude.

My Mama. My Pops (RIP).

My youngins: De'Vondrick Bankston. Diamond Bankston.
Teyonna Moore. Shakeris Bankston.

My grandyoungins: Teondre Smith. Cardier Smith.
Dior Bankston.

My godyoungin: Mi Amor Adelina Bella Harrison.

Sister Tina Hogle. You believed & encouraged.
Pushed & pressed. Sketched & designed. You adamantly
shepherded this project to completion. Thank you.

Family

Circle

Comrades

Each of you who have stepped into and
shared in my struggle and contributed
to my survival and successes.

i

am

We

Introduction.. 7

I. buried alive ~

Mama.. 10
The Mask Way... 12
My World…... 16
Sounding Off.. 18
Genesis 15:20 20
Affliction 22
Shattered 24
Compass.. 27
Dying Times 29
Dry Bones 30
Imagine 31
Reruns... 32
Rise Up 34
Black and Blues... 37
Bootlegged 39
Prayed Up 41
Ripple Effects.. 44
Grace 45
If We Must Die '08 Remix 46
Sight Unseen 48
HERE i AM 51
Beast Mode 57
The Gathering.. 59

II. lost chronicles ~

Origins 62
Be Queen... 65
Juneteenth 69
A Word to Y'All (Part 1).. 70
A Word to Y'All (Part 2).. 73
Me, Rebel Seed 75

Hip Hopocrisy 77
Wondering 79
The Lost Chronicles 80
Heard 'Em Cry 87
Dystopia 88
Feedback 90
Better 92

III. what you know 'bout love? ~

On Auto Pilot 94
Convicted 95
4bit10 96
Overblown 98
Then Became Eve 99
Drawn 100
Snapshots 102
Release 106
Agency 108
Tipsy 109
What You Know 'Bout Love? 110
Bars that Hold 114
A 21 Word Love Story 116
Let It Burn 117
Yours and Mine 118

IV. gathering the pieces ~

A Lonely Place 121
Echoes of You 122
The North Star 124
Residuals 125
Tragicomedy 126
Animal Instincts 128
No Revisions 129
Spoken 130
Compromised 131
Dear Mirror 132

introduction ~

what does a 22 year-old manchild
on his 3rd calendar in bondage
braving a life bid
buried alive
do with his time & his traumas?
he writes
he writes out his woes
tears
nightmares
pipe dreams
wounds
awareness
love
rage
confusion
regrets
self–righteousness
righteous indignation
aspirations
falsehoods
truth
reality
fantasies
he writes his way
from tragic to magic moments…

he writes his damn heart out
in hopes that it will bounce back whole
or
at the very least
strengthen into healing the broken pieces
that he's able to salvage from the breakage

During my 3rd year of captivity, i marched into the library in
Green Bay Max Prison one afternoon on business: i wanted to

Roderick 'Rudy' Bankston   ~

write poetry. i sought out the "inmate" worker on duty and asked if they had any books that supported my mission. Without missing a beat he gestured for me to follow. i listened as he pulled books off the shelves and shared that he wrote poetry. i flooded him with questions, and he generously offered up answers, advice and encouragement. i went back to my cell afterwards, browsed through the books and picked up a pen and got to it.

That same night i wrote my first poem in the south cell hall on f-tier — can't recall the cell number. i thought it was a classic. In retrospect, it was sentimental cornballery. The one copy that i have doesn't want to be found and i understand why. At the same time, i appreciate it because it launched me into poetry as another form of expression, a survival skill, and the pathway toward healing.

Tonight, as i write this intro in my living room, bare feet kicked up on the couch, laptop on my lap, fan blowing comforting air over my legs, i overhear the roars of a storm rumble outside my window. Sounds beautiful. Musical. The contrast dawns on me as it brings to mind the nights i spent in a cell, a storm of voices raging over the tier and in my head, full of provocation for me to yell out for them all to please shut the fuck up. Now the quiet evokes deep appreciation. Another contrast: i am now in my third year of freedom on the verge of finalizing a manuscript of poetry penned over a 20 year span inside the soul crushing machine called the Wisconsin prison system. This year also landed me back in the plus column of freedom. Arrested at eighteen, released at thirty-eight and today forty-one, i have now spent more time walking the earth free than buried alive.

i continue to write because i need to write to make sense of the past, the now, and to heal into tomorrow. i am still salvaging my broken pieces, trying to gather myself into wholeness.

A luta continua,
Roderick 'Rudy' Bankston
September 2018

buried alive

*we reach out for air
and come up empty-handed*

Mama

I.

it took The Fire This Time
for me to intuit my moment
of delivery
your love the incubator
premature how i let slip from memory
the tears that prayed down your cheeks
holy water that baptized me into existence
i (born a false prophecy of joy)
would become obscene spasms in the center
of your gravity
adrift
toward oblivion
engrossed in later term self-abortion

II.

it seems this bridge i invested in
burns and caves in underfoot
flames lick away my costume
the smoke spells out, 'arSONist'
accusing me

below a river of tears testifies
convicting me
you walk its surface
ready to catch me in another trial
your M.O. when it comes to your baby
but this tribulation is too grown
deliverance mandates i man-up

III.

still i will always call you
miracle worker
healer
1st luv
'Black Mother Woman'
evidence of The Great I Am's affection
proof of God's grace
fertile grounds for celebration
glory glory hallelujah

The Mask Way

here in the burial chambers of this Max Prison
we entombed captives live out bigger lies
than we did in the streetz
　　We
　　　　Wear
　　　　　　The
　　　　　　　　Mask
to stash feelings of dysfunction
brokenness
fear
&
defeat
empty of empathy
we reach out for air and come up empty–handed
we cast stones that crumble into sandstorms
&
shower our hypocrisy
down
　　on
　　　　our
　　　　　　heads
we siphon off sips of knowledge
quote powerful excerpts
grow locks & Arabic beards

strut like pharisees
&
feign newfound righteousness
as if being Cyclops in this blind land
certifies our unilateral enthronement
we exist & look alive in the congested midst of zombies
grown little boys lashing out
brimming with misogyny
still angry at mommy for being imperfect
&
perfectly human
childmen boohooing the sinful sprinkles in her eyes
w/out outgrowing the victim–minded cesspool
they're drowning in themselves
submerged
mad at the world for turning w/out them
their own kids living & learning w/out them
spilling libation from the same cups of woes for them
&
i sit fitted in sackcloth & ashes right w/them
our children shortchanged by our shortcomings
i am them
take a gander at us:
simpletons in complex clothing
fraught with self–loathing

upholding synthetic crosses
facades for our double crosses
we are faithfully unwilling to crucify our Jesus Complexes
30 shekel scheming w/Judas reflexes
sounding foolish to the unfooled
prime example is ol' school
this old dude is damn near fifty
still clutching exaggerated memories of his dayz of glory
jappin' about stories that likely never happened
jackin' his state slacks
poppin' his state collar
lookin' pathetic in his OG posture
a str8 up boss impostor
refusing to grow up out of the dead skin that has him
dying within
washed–up & steady lyin'
mostly to himself
sellin' an image... nobody's buyin'
except this young dumb nigga sitting HSED deficient in class
ranting & raving about avenging the recent killing of a friend
huffing
puffing
blowing hot wind
ignoring the trouble he's in
chummy with the ignorance that got him in this grave

mummified & peacocking like he's really 'bout it
&
standing on something
knowin' depressingly well that he ain't standing on nothing
ain't standing on nothing but count
always bickering with Akh' who sits behind him
professing the oneness of Allah
with the same tongue he splits into a fork
&
slams into the exact brotha's back he salaam'd last Friday
at Jum'ah
right before they performed two 2 rak'ahs
peace be unto those of you offended
but this poem won't be rescinded 2 spare the feelings
of kafirs in sanctified garb
some truth gets hard to swallow
harder to stomach & digest
especially when it chokes the ego & bedevils the chest
but once it gets heavy enough inside us
we become strong enough to clean up this mess
we're trapped in

My World...

walls of unflinching concrete
steel doors swollen with confinement that confine me
renamed 249669* to dehumanize and redefine me
the ghost of freedom lurking
taking sick pleasure in reminding me
of loss
slowly losing my mind
letting go
almost gone but holding on
heart heavy and suffering daily heartbreak
engaged in psychological gladiation each waking day
guttural screams permeate the wretched air
segregation
inside
segregation
where voiceless men voice their despair
each day any way noise can be created
a walking dead segment left overly medicated
some diehards remain dead–i–cated
to embattled 'hoods that barely know their names
and
to gangs that left their homies imprisoned
smoked out
or
slain

soul-snatching pain breaks down the hardest "thugs"
no longer idolizing a deathstyle they once loved
— now christianized
or kneeling on a rug — praying eastward five times a day
a slight space given to exist in
to spend the bulk of days and nights in
on a hard bunk
staring at the ceiling
forearm resting on the forehead
aching...for freedom
laughter
beautiful women
did i fail to mention...
this is my world

*prison identification number

Sounding Off

fears foreshadow the next chapter
while so–and–so chase after the hereafter
thru simulated escape routes
cop ya ticket at the nearest death house
smoke the strangler
inhale the polite squeeze
taste the disgrace
tempered by what might please
existing tenuously
watching the earth cave in
schools microwaving their curriculum
to calibrate upgradeable victims
the constipation thickens
once the misinformation gets chopped & screwed up
into miseducation
then chewed up & swallowed to render the mind hollow
thoughts waterboarded in shallow water
too drenched in nonsense to paddle harder
let alone push us to return to our alma maters
& cremate the texts from which they taught us
to denude the nudity of how it scarred us
our brains bastardized by the pretty pale lies
the handiwork of modern day neanderthals in disguise
their abracadabra keeps us hypnotized
scandalized by base ties to this morbid planet

DO NOT pardon me if i sound disenchanted
i'm merely describing the devil–station
it is pivotal that i stay candid in sizing up its expansion
revelation lives under seal in it
but we're too ill in the spirit to understand it
too busy taking God's grace for granted
like it is something we've earned
meanwhile as the world turns
crashes
&
burns
time ages in this land of wastage
where the sages sell out for trinkets & slave wages
they ignore the writing on the wall & try to rewrite
the pages
of God's love
but let me tell ya what God loves:
the sinner in the back pew who's genuine in his messiness
the saint in the front pew who's humble in her blessedness
both in the fellowship of the faithful
yearning for forgiveness

Genesis 50:20

The knell of death resounds
throughout the valley
feet planted on the narrow path
in motion
battle fatigued
shadowboxing with satan's silhouette
bobbing at the bottom
weaving through the wilderness
thirsty in Horeb
licking rocks that shed fervent tears
weeping Jesus in my ears
visions of salvation floundering on water
The Father
the sons
can't forget about the Daughters
Proverbs 31 Sistahs in the valley
their crucified wombs birth blessings
the lost articles of faith lie coffined
in wounds
the sacred enclosed in
the demise of self
the Spirit roused in
atonement
war waged against the flesh
of my flesh

bone of my bone marrow
blood of my bloodline
in the valley
tired
caving
fallin'
stripped of my robe and royal lineage
by hands sanitized in treachery
crestfallen in the downfall
tracking ancestral footsteps
inside the cistern
trapped in self
strengthened
reading Joseph's insignia on the walls closing in
flashing signs of hope
in the blackout
opportunities for redemption
in the affliction
it was written
anointment for dry bones
in the valley
this valley is a breeding ground
for warriors...

Affliction*

as these fogged days fade away
under the suffocation of lonely nights
i muster with all my might the fortitude to hold on
to this fragile thread of hope
wavering inside me
praying earnestly for the Most High to guide me
through this dazed existence
where at every instance i awaken to fall
into a Nightmare
the flaring glare of despair stares hatred
without abatement
i soldier my way out of debasement
each slippery stair a mile long
i pray past broken men craving home
as torment attaches itself to every breath
i breathe
i grieve
but see better dayz smiling at me
from a distance
i climb
i crawl
i claw my way towards its fulfillment
faith compelling me

spirit propelling me
forward
onward
i am here to survive
and rise up out of this abyss
scathed but unbroken

Written my first day in Supermax, Boscohell Wisconsin.

Shattered

I.

i exist in fragments
living
buried
above the underground
overgrown in my 30's
alone
&
crowded with a vacant expression
in my awareness of past mishaps
present misgivings about
life
death
the here
the now

II.

tomorrow happened yesterday morning
evening out the pros and cons
of consciousness

III.

sleep is complex
i yearn for rest

peace
&
paradise
on this road to perdition
driven from nowhere below me
going somewhere slow

IV.

i possess a license to heal
from the damage done at conception
precocious misconceptions
never taught me how to untangle what strangled me
starting with the umbilical cord
all i ever wanted to do is breathe on my own

V.

i sense the sun
in the darkest recesses of my interior—
brilliant
defiant
enlightenment enters through these wounds
to remind me to treat life like it's
my only begotten son

VI.
only i am i
a unique figment of God's imagination
manifested in the flesh
vital fluid
bone
marrow
mystic force

Compass

I.
what mere man can measure another man's worth?
no technological advance can reproduce the earth
in its totality
GPS is virtual reality
in the real scheme of things
find your own way

II.
it's futile to Google the future
better to save it
from the 'great minds of today'
it's best to fear God
&
never trust the man that demands you not question
while encouraging you to walk blindly
before him
beside him
behind him
fall in line behind his ass and
kick it up out of his ego

III.
saying what matters doesn't matter
is deadlier than anti–matter
if our principles contrast with what we practice
we become mere actors on the stage of life
awaiting the curtain call
once the curtain falls
it is curtains on what we coulda
shoulda
woulda
become

Dying Times

Horrid crimes like the old times
But no hanging noose this time
Choice of weapon: black nines
No white sheet wearer this time
Hunted and lynched by our own kind
His skin tone is black as mine
So why can't we seem to find
A realer reason and rhyme
To revamp the paradigm
Of Willie Lynch's design
Keep them coming in soup lines
To create more frankinsteins
Crack smoke floats to the skyline
Befogging all the sunshine
Clouding the spirit and mind
This sick genocidal grind
Got us greedily inclined
Then eventually confined
To prison with space–age time
Or prematurely flatlined
Souls sold for nickels and dimes
To satan as he reclines
Back and sips his savage wine
While God's children keep dying

Dry Bones

Pic #1
a snapshot of simple joy
is worth a thousand rough drafts
as long as the final write captures
what only a smile can and words can't
say, 'cheese!'

Pic #2
overgrown since children
anonymous Sistahs transmogrify N2 statues
— standing out of grasp —
2 protect what's left
of the little girl's innocence within
their passion 2 break free
2 be–come whole & unafraid

Pic #3
under the weight of a restless soul
thoughts fall flat N2 valleys
where Ezekiel prophesies over the dry bones
of slain poets who catch their breath in spirit
and convert their graves so life can live
even when blood spills and dreams are left for dead
God is Good

Imagine

imagine havin' ya dreams shattered
b4 ya drift 2 sleep
&
poison poured in ya gray matter
causing ya 3rd eye to weep
with ya heart knee–deep in sorrow
&
the tides are rapidly rising
ya try'na float N2 2morrow
while feelin' ya boat capsizing
visualizing ya self planting seeds in acid rain
hopin' rose petals spring 4th 2 decorate ya pain
as faith strains 2 push through the steel of ya soul
thoughts frappéed by the chill of the cold
watchin' each day erode
'til daybreak dawns 2 mock ya existence
de–spite all that shit U tackle the new horizon
as the windstorm roadblocks ya resistance
...imagine it

Reruns

My subconscious smells
noxious. Musty reveries.
Inklings with funky hygiene.
Psyche stuck on split screen.
CLICK. CLICK.
Viewing in 3D
scenes of the future lying
under the guillotine
blade on bling
threatening to behead
long overdue dreams
in default, unredeemed.
CLICK.
Vision gangrened
dis–eased
immune to vaccines.
CLICKETY CLICK.
Seeing 1st hand
grown men wheezing
walking dead
fiending for a flight
to escape another night
of trauma

blunted & haunted by
bad karma
memories fraught with
drama galore
canker sores plaguing their
inner core
stumbling thru the morgue
on their thousandth death
still dying
hobbling toward the grave
still trying to sway
the undertaker to take
them under
buried alive in hunger
feeling no stronger
CLICK CLICKETY CLICK.
PASS THE REMOTE!
CLICKCLICKCLICKCLICK
CHANGE THE FUCKIN' CHANNEL!
CLICK. SOMEBODY TiVO HOPE! CLICK...
Static…………….

Rise Up

You damn right i tote these weapons
words that wither bars & chisel chains into ash heaps
the game's deep
so i dig into the depths of me
to glean totemic treasures incapable of measure
to apply pressure
my wordplay is enemy of the state

See!
while Big Brother propagates
images of our fraternal killings
i expose how they hook our babies on Ritalin —
deadly narcotics clothed in therapeutic pharmaceuticals
Come on & go on this tour
let's explore the subtle tug–of–war
& its blatant implications for tomorrow's generations
It's convoluted but not all that complicated
& if we must converse thru these verses to be heard
— then so be it
Maybe we need to APB ourselves
'cause we went on the run from the cause
before effecting true change
gone missin' betwixt last night's tragedy
&
this morning's agony

stuck

in

between

What the fuck is a dream

when a king can't sleep at night

& a Queen has lost all self–esteem & insight

blinded by and bound to moonshine under moonless skies

illumined with manufactured sunlight

that's doomed to flicker & fizzle out

clouds that drizzle out brimstone

Listen On!

i'm talkin' about Man's internal nature

the hidden storms

Best believe true Jihad is raging

within our flesh & bone temples

its psychological shock–and–awe

blowing our senses to smithereens

so i ward off the coup de grace

with truth pouring from my pen like kerosene

to flame what i mean into the minds of the masses

no subterranean whispers

i blast it when i broadcast this

Spark a conflagration thru out the nation

the hemisphere

the globe
stoke that FIRE NEXT TIME
'til it blazes out of 'their' control
torch those watered–down versions
while casting iconoclastic aspersions on the ones
most deserving
pyropoetics!

Burn, baby, burn!
rage against the machine
we'll bear this cross in the spirit of Simon the Cyrene...

Rebel!
til we hear freedom ring...
Rebel!
til we see freedom ring...
Rebel!
til we feel freedom ring...

Black 'n Blues

The Blues is tears shed like Muddy Waters
soakin' the empty seat at my daughter's basketball game
got me staggering in these chains
down the hall of shame
you sho' you wanna know 'bout this here thang
called The Blues?
i doubt it'll amuse you
but it'll definitely disabuse you of those uncircumcised notions
about The Blues of Black folks
The Blues coast on the turbulent waters of our emotions
The Blues run deep as the Atlantic Ocean
The Middle Passage
Maafa
Africa's Greatest Disaster
hatin' historians insinuating that this past doesn't at all matter!

The Blues is a people shattered
their identities left in tatters
preacher man preachin' some pie in the sky:
"Obey ya Master...reward cometh in the hereafter"
biblical backstabbers
The Blues is solo
collective
respectful
regretful
workable
&
gets deep down–in–the–corridors–of–ya–heart personal

The Blues

The Blues is separation from the few lovin' me
The Blues is my Mama huggin' me
with sorrow in her eyes as we kiss goodbye
she prayin' that I get free & make it home
before she makes it home to that "Sweet By 'N By"
The Blues is demonic despair & the audacity of hope
a way that we cope
The Blues is the Blue Note manifesting in Nina Simone's throat
that Can't Stop Won't Stop Negro Spirituals
ragtime
reggae: "No Woman, No Cry"
Bessie Smith's "Cold in Hand Blues"
vocals on fire with The Blues

The Blues

The Blues is weary toe taps
cotton–splintered finger snaps
honey hips swingin' that brown–round all around
juke joint 'Color Purple' rumbles... it's goin' down
throwin' 'bows inna club
like what!
screaming "Don't Shoot!" wit' both hands up
The Blues is fuel–efficiency
WMD on our enemy
includin' "in–a–me"
The Blues is guttural deep bittersweet melodies

Bootlegged

absurd scenes of bootlegged Blackness
stream across TV screens & leap into the eyes
plaguing the minds of our children
feeding them warped images
of themselves
potential giants con–verted to elves
scales jailing their pineal glands
making it hard for them to understand
that their Afrikan roots salute their spirits
& melanin beautified their skin when it filled it
'cause God willed it
sadly the tragedy:
too many know more about clubbin' & thuggin'
than Black on Black lovin' & Harriet Tubman
the ancients must cry the Nile River
Hurricane Katrina tears fall
watchin' the struggle stall as we fall
LIKE victims
to J. Edgar Hoover's system
"Not God Bless" him
GOD DAMN him!
& his dragged–out use of COINTELPRO to
kidnap
murder
frame

& imprison
"Black messiahs" — fearing our rising
the same ol' frame–work
with the same ol' frame–ups
robbing us of the epitome of i am WE
so the sleepin' giant stays in a comatose state
snoring
tossing
turning
on the verge of dying
on the verge of dying
in its sleep
we are dying
in
our
sleep

Prayed Up

at the dusk of dawn i dig for my Rosetta stone
yearning for self exegesis before Jesus comes
i plumb the recesses of my essence & far beyond
experiencing a kinship with the Cross & the Crescent
where do i belong
what must i become to become among the heirs
of the kingdom when The Kingdom comes
i dread being left untaken
left behind
left alone
forsaken
i just wanna make it...to that eternal home
where the offspring of God can roam
freely
&
take in pictures of Scripture painted untainted vividly
brought to actuality without the misery
the past the backdrop
history as the baptistery
but that's faith in things unseen
the present is the reality
in it i pen this rhapsody
call me Mister Slaveboat Survivor
slave survivor sensibilities is an ark of floetry floating thru me
mustards seeds sown under divine husbandry
mercy mercy me

reflections of the sun linger from
when this one Sistah took a shine to me
she spoke love to me
said, "Young brotha, ya Black & gifted..."
but i wouldn't listen — i didn't listen to her wisdom
instead i fed her drug addiction
now my heart bleeds for forgiveness
hers and God's
prayerful and repentant
for neglecting
Naw! for degrading our upliftment
i contributed by tarnishing Black Gold
no longer minimizing my role
it is real
so Israel
wrestling with the angel like Jacob
this life sentence & a wake–up
sometimes make me not wanna wake up
still i wake up
prayed up & take up my cross
Lord knows it's hard to make up for lost time
with a lost mind
demons whispering bribes to leave me beholden
to suicide
but the devil is a lie!
that is why i rebuke & refuse satanic bargains

the devil's clapping at the core of my faith
i was born his target
for my son & my daughters
willingly i'll die a martyr
please bless 'em, Holy Father
to draw farther into Your Light
i pray You make 'em sharper
so they dig further in life

Ripple Effects

Shh…listen…
to the snickers in the winds
trickling thru the ether
taunting our attempts to probe the perplexity
of life on earth
our 3rd eyes dilate in wonder at conundrums
caked in cryptic matter
shrouded in metaphor — unsolvable on the surface
enigmas we're unable to unscramble
the decoders lie entombed inside nullified children
pregnant with promise
rendered broken
left breathless & beyond our grasp
their outcries echo beneath the ocean floor
stoking ripples into tsunamis
as their love — a phantom —
aquaplanes on stillborn tears
unable to reach shore
jilted & stranded
abandoned at sea
&
we, twisted in confusion,
we deep–soul dive
only to drown in our efforts to rescue
what we permitted to perish
the clouds thicken…absorbing anguish we caused
the clouds darken…pelting down raindrops
that burst into scornful laughter upon impact

Grace

Lord please grant me the strength
to stand in your light
without losing sight

If We Must Die '08

if we must die…
why not emulate Claude McKay's approach
choke back the schemes of our enemies
with a vehement reproach
coach our progeny to succeed in the end game of revolution
overthrowin' the slave mentality with all its illusions
all its confusions
cease with the snoozin'
reawaken, you mighty race
about-face
&
retrace the historical path traveled
ancient sand in the hourglass
unravels a past stashed in a web of lies
snatch the gossamer off of Heru's eye
envision us fully risen
engulfed in thriven culture
heedin' the wisdom of Sankofa
goin' back to fetch Afrikan intellect
resurrecting love, honor & respect
for those who carried us over
seekin' within for Jehovah
O' if we must die…let it not be over
bloodstained gains or bronze egos
or

muddy silver linings & artificial flavored rainbows
O' comrades, if we must die…
do it for unchained expression of soul
& unbridled power to grow
"get free or die tryin" the motto
showin' us brave
our hearts ablaze
struggle–made
defyin' the grave
givin' our all against the attack
pressed to the wall
but fightin' back!

Sight Unseen

i am not a fluke
i am God's flute
uniquely handcrafted thru His immaculate mastery
Her luv is oxygen i breath on
i sway to the breeze of…. heavenly melody
even as i traverse the rugged terrain of this earthly valley
peopled by people who view without vision
& yes i strive to walk by faith & not by sight
But i also recognize God endowed us with eyes
that includes a reason why
&
sometimes truth gets ugly & sin feels lovely
it is the curse, it is the blessing
so why settle for less than
or open our minds only for the ingestion of
theological placebos that spiritualize
the slaughter of God's people
oppression is evil
satanically instigated
often self–perpetuated
but it's the silence
THE APPALLING SILENCE…
of 'good people' that helps it escalate
&
blows open the floodgates
for misguided warriors to come out & play
thinkin' it's okay–kay–kay to squander their youth
in pursuit of status symbols

like Cadillac Escalades on oversized blades
pulling overpriced shades down over their face
tinting their 3rd eye blind
existing without reason
dying…out of season
it's an earsplitting act of treason to practice silence…
or make gavels out of our tongues & judge the young
someone anyone tell 'em
befo' Soulja Boy Tell 'Em to supersoak a Sistah's image of self
with the ho spiel of death
someone anyone tell 'em that even in the jaws of defeat
there can still be victory
&
that ignorance is the worst form of tyranny
someone anyone tell 'em
that every miracle need not be empirical
many are manifest in the spiritual realm
someone anyone tell them that it's about repentance
it's about redemption
&
any set of ambitions minus those two are just about senseless
like fear is senseless
unless it's reverential
i question any negro's credential who is timid in his mental
fearful of knowledge that rocks
& shocks
& hurts
& reworks his understanding up to a better standing

who shuns truth that lets loose our pent–up anger & shame
&
Christlike passion to speak in flames of truth to power
no matter how powerful
some would rather be cowards though
&
demonize the folks who roll up their sleeves
to plant freedom seeds
&
uproot the insidious weeds of white supremacy
they cherish western theology
when they should feel embarrassed & demand an apology
justice
&
liberty
if not that trinity then 'So What!'
woe is us if we lose our minds try'na love…racists
covert or blatant in their hatred
listen how they speak with condescension
whenever in their presence
INCOMING MESSAGE:
i will never do the Bojangles
i'd rather be strangled
by the very hands of those who came before me
who stood up before me
they stood up for you
they stood up for me
so that we will know how to stand
& know what to stand for

HERE i AM

Written by Revolutionary Comrades:
Dyzae Kemet (David Crowley,1979–2002)
Trone Kemet, (Kashanti Kisis Kemet 1979–2002)
Rudy Kemet (Roderick V. Bankston)

DYZAE:
HERE i AM, wiping coal out of my eyes
awakened by information that was denied,
and purposely unwritten & untold
to keep us asleep from truth
but knowledge was the key that unlocked
the chains to my brain
giving me the power to secure our future
by reaching the youth
Many died fighting apartheid —
they studied for years but when it
was time, put the books aside,
stood their ground & took action.
I live in the spirit of Nat Turner,
Fred Hampton, Lil Bobby Hutton,
Huey P. Newton, Jonathan & George Jackson.
Now HERE i AM, A Revolutionary with a cause —
with a vision of great change,
one who will fight even though "they"
don't fight fair.
Yes, So HERE i AM, willing to die

for what I believe in, but at times
I wonder did Doctor King have a dream or a nightmare....

TRONE BONE:
HERE i AM, a breathing, capable,
intelligent human being,
deprived, degraded, discouraged, & threatened,
so I won't speak out against the wrong
that I'm seeing. Can you feel
the knife as it cuts,
the rope as it chokes,
the whip as it licks,
at my beautiful skin????
Do you think our prayers will be answered,
our cries will be heard,
our efforts will succeed
on hope that we will rightfully win?
Do you see the land we have structured,
the sights we have built,
and the technology we have modernized?
Do you know of the spittings, beatings,
rapes, murders, mental abuse, social abuse,
economical abuse; and that the orchestrators
of this never apologized???
But instead they modernized slavery
with their laws, jails, false educational
systems, advertisement of false leaders,
false law enforcement: judges, lawyers,

police, mayors, presidents, and deprivation of
opportunity.
They love the Black on Black crime,
negative music, Black dope dealers, Black pimps,
Black broken homes, Black discouraged, misled,
uneducated children, and our fucked up
community!!!!

KASHANTI:

HERE i AM, struggling through another day —
A struggle for my brothaz, for my Sistaz,
A struggle for my people,
I watch the news and it's Black on Black crime,
I read the paper and it's Black on Black crime,
and I look at the system and it's Blacks who
get the most time.
We are being deprived of the truth people!
I ask myself who controls the MEDIA?
Who writes the newspapers?
Who runs the courts?
COINCIDENCE?
Or is this evidence of the many injustices
being spoonfed to our people? It is NECESSARY
for us to bring down this wall of mental and
social despair — we will do this BY ANY MEANS.
Being free physically does not exist when you
are mentally enslaved (ABRAHAM KNEW THAT).
The doors of opportunity for the youth in

the ghetto have been locked for so long by
discrimination, we've given up looking for
the key of EQUALITY.
But the kids in middle America possess the
skeleton key — But don't mention that because
now we've touched on something else —
We've shed light on the dark corners
they don't want us to see.
That's a conspiracy!
When will we stop paying the debt?
We're all paying it with our blood, sweat & tears.
But the crazy thing is, we haven't borrowed a thing!

RUDY KEMET:
HERE i AM,
trudging this road of broken chains and blood stains
listening to the winds gently hum Harriet Tubman's name
i strain my ears to listen as i vaguely hear:

"She escaped, went back, escaped and went back
until her aching feet turned numb...so, Blackman,
every time you escape don't forget where you come from."

HERE i AM,
surveying the footprints embedded in the terrain
epic relics of altruistic sacrifices — so priceless

HERE i AM,

awakening out of mental slumber
yawning into awareness
"Keep moving," the winds murmur. *"The chains
will be torn asunder."*

STILL HERE i AM,
wondering, 'What Chains?' Then i hear,
*"Don't be fooled...the Emancipation Proclamation
is a false claim
feel the heaviness of your brains*!"

HERE i AM,
indignant
as my mind grimaces at the falsehoods
and becomes decolonized into consciousness
finding myself in deep thought
thinking, *"What is this?"* as i bear witness

HERE i AM,
intrigued while becoming immersed in what i am ignorant of
and also seem to recognize
hearing stories of Black giants that leave me mesmerized

HERE i AM,
standing at the scratch line
defiant and ready to crossover
onto this lonely road
i've been called to travel

Black Family,
Here We Are
because of what we've been through
and what we become will be the result
of how far we're willing to go
to reach ourselves and live free

Beast–Mode

Inspect the source of the text
to avoid the con put in the text
put it in con–text when they stress that the
meek shall inherit the earth
store up ya treasures in Heaven
there's no pleasure in inheriting dirt
existing on both knees
head down
crashing to the ground — mind first
murked worst
Lawd, my stomach hurts
someone get me some pepto
FAST!
i'm lactose intolerant
&
these milquetoast knee–grows give me gas
trip the feces out of me
done upholstered their chains in chinchilla
& claimed they ain't never been so free
Naw nigga! you ain't ever been so asleep
unable to tweak that rattle in ya heartbeat
it holds no rhythm with the ones who march to the drumbeat
of Sistah Shirley Chisholm
She stayed unbossed & unbought
while too many of us stay lost
& bought off

caught off guard while they shade us

much love to our Earthshines

Warrior women sublime like Ms. Angela Davis

for strivin' to save us

never went shuckin' 'n jivin' with those who enslaved us

uprooted & engraved us

broke & remade us in the image of chattel

beast of burden — saddled

treated worse than cattle

whipped....with cowhide and shit

now we ride whips & boast 'bout being beasts

not peepin' the disturbing irony

drop a grip to make our paint do acrobatic flips

but won't flip the script & quit using past abuses as excuses

to do nothing but keep fakin'

like ours is the only generation

that's felt forsaken at one time or another

it is time to awaken to our greatness

& get this earth shaking

The Gathering

Poet, Bless Your Name —

1st i'll testify to how it be–came
Stolen Legacy blasphemed into unknown infamy
Dragged thru the mud of occidental archaeology
X–factor in my pedigree
the origins of primordial x–men emergin' against the sands
The lost clan of Abra–Ham
Nomads who lost track of Moses
Pharaoh slipped my lineage a lethal dosage of hocus–pocus
To knock us comatose
Lifeless inna identity crisis
Inna dark 'bout who Christ is
Divested of what we came with
Our inheritance of intuitive testimonials
Inscribed on ancestral memorials
i finally grasped what the oracles spoke
Paid homage and reverted to the rebirth
of Bellicose 'No–Saint' Kemet
scion of divine intellect

From Where You Have Came —

Thru the annals of perdition
Buck City, WisConviction
The locale where ALEXIS PATTERSON went MISSING!!!
That Amber Alert must've malfunctioned on her

GIVE US BACK OUR CHILDREN!!!
A ransom i will give 'em
one worse than Mel Gibson's
polar opposite to anything fiction
no treasure–trove at the end of that artificial rainbow coalition
The hood's in critical condition
off life support sans health care
in culture shock...no defibrillation
no child support...no welfare
only the mirage of the crystal stairs 'round here
i solemnly swear fo' Gawd
it's a helluva swindle down @ Potawatomi Casino
LOCATIONLOCATIONLOCATION
in the cleavage of the colony
BINGO!
snitchin' subbin' at a crescendo
Obamanomic holice (SIC) state
the abysmal graduation rate is the segue to the prison gates
another Mother of color at her baby's wake
who's to say what we die for
Only thing fa' sho' is that we die
the same way we're born
premature
America's veiled metaphor

lost chronicles

Pyramids in the rear view of an
edited history
defaced monuments in the mirror
disfigured reflections
uprooted bodies fettered & filched
& shipped over raving waters
sharks lurking underneath the
crimson tides
filthy with holocaust

Roderick 'Rudy' Bankston   ~

Origins

i am Blackman
African
Christian praising Allah
in Jehovah's synagogue

i am Kemetic kith
creating mysteries
unfathomable
for eons and eons

my mind's eye reflects the neon
gleaming from my soul
my history holds in its grip
the beginning of mankind

my Father's fingertips
massaged Eden's soil
before he planted me in her garden
i spring forward saturated in innocence
and a spittin' image of His Holy Spirit

rich deposits of promise
ferment in me
propelling me forward
i tread paths pointed toward
destiny

i stumble on the auction block
of slavery
after enemies' ships carried me
then denied me what my charity
taught them

i am ashy field hands
furtively molding freedom
i am nurturer of Nat Turners
and Toussaint L'Ouvertures
when i feed them strange fruit
plucked from an historical tree
rooted in ancient glory

i am temple brimming
with revolutionary tuition
hieroglyphics are carved in my walls
my words transmit their truth

i am voice of the blues
jazz
bebop
and hip hop
lost in poetry

i hone my misery into a weapon
steppin' in my boots

affirming my roots
as my brother shoots at my flesh
w/out realizing it's his own

i am what's gone in me
and
what's unknown about me

i am the kidnapped sum and substance
buried in the spiritual basement
of the gangsta and drug addict
and thug acting melodramatic

i am dormant greatness inside of a dying
breed
frantically trying to breathe
i am me
i am we
i am us
i am Blackman
African

Be Queen

Last night i stumbled
upon a sacred scroll hidden inside my subliminal
the words written stoked my pulse
i felt fallacies dwindle
the love rekindle
earthshine sprung thru the window of my soul
as i decoded each primal line inside my mental abode
my meditations spoke
i awoke to ancient echoes of: "Be Queen…"
this mantra left resonating intimately within my innermost
provoking my muse
so i gracefully arose
grabbed pen & paper & wrote:

Dear Beloved Black Woman
i beseech you to please… Be Queen
it's rooted in ya Afro–genes
the flow supreme in ya bloodstream
tap into the blessed energy
stiff–arm those schemes waged against ya esteem
and…Be Queen

Original Madonna be–coming
Eve's seed returning
embrace the goddess essence
that is yours
that is yours
that is yours and… Be Queen

Roderick 'Rudy' Bankston   ~

The Sistahs with vision
struggling to pay school tuition
those in corporate Amerikkka head–butting the glass ceiling
brimming with ambition on a phenomenal mission
stay purpose driven and... Be Queen

The Sistahs hittin' the highway strippin'
the Ones burger flippin
9 to 5 giggin'
always givin' but rarely gettin'
keep on keepin' on
keep on building and... Be Queen

The Sistahs locked in the bowels of the beast
hurting for release
searching for peace of mind
&
trying to recapture the shattered pieces of mind
Y'all will be just fine
so just... Be Queen

The Sistahs biddin' on death–row
diggin' for ya Underground Railroad
in full Harriet Tubman mode
standing firm on weary toes
listen up close
grab yo' hammer & chisel & dig this here
hear this clear: Be Queen!

The Black Girls lost & rejected
the AIDS infected
the cancerous breasted
Y'all who crawled thru dark periods of being molested
Sistah, you're still worthy
your self–esteem is still wealthy
you're still royalty
so sashay on to destiny and... Be Queen

The same goes for the Sistahs raped
&
traumatized
who came forward then got accused of telling lies
& strung up & crucified in the public's eye
Still you rise
Still you rise
Still you... Be Queen

The Sistahs who fled the flood
when the levees blew up
y'all tossed by Katrina
brushed off by FEMA
left to die but grew gills & survived
hold your head high!
SO High! and... Be Queen

The bounty hunted Sistahs
(Assata in exile)
the political targets who do us proud

who showed us how to stand firm
under the gun
the Mama & Daddy wrapped up in one
Awesome Flesh of Femininity
the backbone of our community
your love is our remedy
so please continue to... Be Queen

But wait...
it'll be betrayal to forget
the Sistahs nursing the sick
in the midst of the Darfur Conflict
starving for wheat
thirsty for peace
our pain runs deep
i curse this beast
'cause i am We
i Am WE!
and beautiful Sistahs, we need y'all to...
BE QUEENS!

Juneteenth

Fast-Forward: 21st Century.
RIP Ralph Ellison. Penned prophecy.
A people google their identity.
Invisible man abased in the basement.
The foundation of civilization.
Juneteenth celebration's a no-go.
The 40 acres. The mules. All a no-show.
No land. No power. No dough.
Black Folks sacrificed their lives to vote.
Vote or Die. Slick quotes.
Dreams peddled at the polls. Recounts so
our voices won't count. Loopholes.
Ante-up out of slavery. This is Cutthroat
Capitalism. A footnote. Teenage amendments are
never enough. Still broke. The number 13 ain't
brought us a bit of luck. Add it up.

A Word to Ya'll
(Part 1)

Ida B. Wells,
    if you could see the scene now
    ain't no tellin' how many cracks
    would cringe ya heart apart
    i grimace as i mention the new wave lynchings
    &
    how some colored women have suspended sight
    of their origins
    &
    the bestowed mission
    permitting their gorgeous image to be blemished
    &
    noosed in High Definition
    promotin' a burlesque fiction of the brainless black vixen

Ms. Ida B.,
    i know your vision never envisioned me in a prison
    locked & languishing under crushing confinement
    shame reigns in me
    over fallin' ignorantly to the back of the bus
    tainting the trust that you invested in us
    i apologize
    contrition drenching the eye of my soul

now they use criminal convictions
to disenfranchise Black folks
&
due to conditioning
some who can, still won't vote
opting to gripe rather than fight
to make things right
trampling on the sacrifices given that kept us livin'

Sistah Ida,
    i feel a nippy breeze swirling all around
    freezing the maltreated blood on the leaves
    as strange fruit swing in
    a
    wild
    fall
    from poplar trees
    plummeting into casualties
    unripe tragedies left to spoil in the streets
    their young lives lost
    snuffed out
    rushed out of existence
    i hear Billy Holiday's soft whispers
    cruise the whirlwinds
    her lady–blue vibes trying to re–attune us

to the truth of our bruised roots
we're cut off from the life source
unable to grow the collective
into one whole people
although we could

A Word to Ya'll
(Part 2)

Scot La Rock,
    if you saw the state of hip hop now
    ya whole mood would catch a cold crush
    flush in 808 ripples
    until it ruptures
    right
    down
    the
    middle
    it's hardly hunger for the profound found
    no appetites to Boogie Down down
    &
    produce
    the artform lay dozing
    frozen in this Neo–Ice Age
    our Black rage has been whitewashed and led astray
    sucka MCs go out their way
    to dash down the primrose paths
    paved by the ones who laughed at rap in the beginning
    nowadays their progeny keep our music spinnin'
    who would've ever conceived it
    on a global scale fans fiend it
    like they so need it
    while corporate crooks try to bleed it dry

they're quick to crucify
the truth of conscious sound
to keep its message entombed
underground
the slaves who do the Kunta Kinte & run away
get no airplay
still some stay defiant prey
resistant to the vultures' sophisticated attempts
to leave the culture suffocated
seditious lyricists
rebellious in their wordplay
spittin' venom draped in rhythm
sick wit' it — no serum
paradoxical flows delivering the antidotes
prescribed for the world–wide ghetto

Me, Rebel Seed

Me, Rebel Seed forced to grow
from the nappy roots of George Jackson's bloodied afro
the hidden pistol palmed
straight shootin' with no qualms when i pop off
and drop off head–shots tinged with napalm
i write & recite psalms simply to pierce you mentally
reel you in then fill you in
tick tock! no time delays once the Big Bang begins
barreling thru the darkest matter with the starkest light
eclipsed by cognition
shelling out sight beyond sight
epiphanies encoded with 360 degreed views on reality
who in the cosmos really sees thru the blinding–eye
of un/natural catastrophes
in the devil–station
saints & sinners are shaken to their knees
confounded by Revelation
& the 'silence in Heaven'
the world wars to the earthquakes to 9/11
from the 1st seal to the 7th
faith rushed to a standstill by questions:
'is this God's will?' or 'satan's killing fields?'
inner–being spinning
dizzily
descending
downhill

to rock bottom — brought low to steeper dimensions
where revolutionary brain waves signal deeper intentions
boots laced
moving at a heightened pace in lockstep
towards one death
for one cause
all ours
Me, Rebel Seed forced to grow...

Hip Hopocrisy

shush the d–boy poppycock
got our seeds poppin' pills —
chopped
sacrificing their youth onna profane altar of Moloch
high time to synchronize our watch with the eternal tick–tock
of God's biological clock
and teach those who think they know but know not
that their minds bathe in melanin 24/7/365
non stop
an innate stock of chemistry that can't be exhausted with time
rewind to unbind the underrated minds
that are still under appreciated
by those invaders who claimed copyrights
to what Imhotep initiated
if only the ancestors would've barred 'em from the garden
or made 'em depart
before they spewed poison & squeezed so many
thru The Doors Of No Return
the bottom of the Atlantic is our Urn
where ash heaps & bone fragments rest stagnant
so dummy-boy why ya braggin'
pants SAGGIN'
spell that backwards
NIGGA ya backwards
a pro–fessional minstrel show actor
instead of resistance ya doin' Jim Crow's biddin'

while our Political Prisoners are stuck biddin'
>Free Mumia! Free Mutula!
>Free 'em now!
>Free Acoli! Pardon Assata!
>Free 'em all! Freedom Now!

how absurd was The White Man's Burden
Manifest Destiny left us hurtin'
salt keeps pouring in the wounds beneath our whip lashes
some will claim i wasn't there
unaware of my BLACKFLASHES
history drips from Lady Liberty's woolly eyelashes
100 Years Of Lynching congregate on her face
sediments of Amerikkka's shame
but she's not to blame
they gave her a face change & displaced her broken chains
lift up her dress
& her chocolate womb will confess a different tale
than her Amerikkklanized looks & what's in the textbooks
with their watered-down truth splashing the wrong impression
justifying oppression
like we deserve the Bell Curve
they perverted the Hamitic Curse
to deify whiteness
fighting this false supremacy isn't in me
it is on us to decolonize our consciousness
and live in our collective power

Wondering

how do we instill in our children
the notion that the true measure of realness
is based on how well we take care of family

The Lost Chronicles

I.
Pillaged lands tainted by foreign hands
its sun–caressed inhabitants branded soulless savages
their struggle thru the cultural ravages did epic damage to
their balance
left their faculties out of balance…

II.
Pyramids in the rear view of an edited history
defaced monuments in the mirror
disfigured reflections
uprooted bodies fettered
filched
&
shipped over graveyarded water
sharks lurking under the crimson tides
filthy with holocaust
convergent bloodstreams
colliding with gut–wrenching screams
caked in exotic agonies…
Seized by torment
captivated by these anomalies
QUESTION IT! QUESTION IT!

III.
"Hows we's git here
doin' hell froms suns–up

to suns–down?"
performing clandestine rain dances
praying for boll weevil showers
QUESTION THIS! QUESTION THIS!!

IV.
Went from gazing upon Heru–On–The–HORIZON
initiates of The Mysteries
&
alumni of Timbuktu Education
down into, "heathen niggahs worship this
here God–given plantation, pick cotton
till yo fingers rotten..."

"Yes, sir, Massa sir," uttered
as the heart mutters, "catch me's later
if you's can, Godless bastard..."

Late night flights
Northern Star trails
underground
hiked middle fingers to those slave codes…

V.
Then celebration. "Thankin' da good Lawd we'sa
free peoples now fo' sho'!!!"
...then cursing, "these goddamned ghettos..."

(EPISODES THUNDER...
BLACKENING THE EYE OF THE STORM...
FLASHING BACK INTO AWARENESS...)

VI.
Brown eyes ablaze
staring in horror
going blind
never really seeing...it coming

FEELING: dynamite ignite!

four precious babies hated to pieces
blown away
shattered to pieces
forced to rest in peace!
Holy Black Quartet lost in the debris of hatred
desecrated by the sacrilege against their sanctuaries
crashed church crumbled their dreams
martyred into a nightmare
LONG LIVE THEIR DREAMS!

VII.
Freedom Rides
Freedom Rides
Swerving left
Swerving right
Sit–ins at the sit–ins
standing up to stand on what must be stood for...
HEARING: gunfire
fire hosings
KKK–9s barking
salivating

Bull Conner's vitriol: "DIE, NIGGER, DIE!"

DEFIANCE. "The Nigger in me is already deceased.
He died so that i can live, pig."

"WHITE POWER!"

"POWER TO THE PEOPLE!!"

VIII.
"Nigga please..."

"Shut up with that infested word, house nigger!"

"Right on, my brothah."

"Am i yours, Black man?"

Silence…

Quiet before the next storm…

The commotion. "Get ya hand out my pocket!"

The blast of double–barreled betrayal...

"Malcolm, come back!"

"As Salaam Alaikum," greeted the Black Shining Prince.
"I'm right in the souls of Black folks, always."

IX.
Naturals grow bolder
heads lift higher
skin radiates with a deeper hue

SAY IT LOUD: I'M BLACK & I'M PROUD!
"Now, boy, ya bets give me dat other nigger
cheek. Don't go try'na luv ya' self like ya
some white man and actin' uppity
ya hear?"

"Why did we ever listen?"

Clenched fist exalted
Chants of 'Black Power!' amplified
Afros aglow
Aware of the rhetoric of reactionaries
Fearless in the face of fascism

X.
"...Not fearing any man... my
eyes have seen the coming..."

The shot rang out!

Political assassination
State sponsored terror

The cries. "Oh Lawd!"

"Jesus, No!"

The tremors. "King is gone!"

The quakes. "Gone where?"

"To glory..."

The eruption. "Regicide outside the Lorraine Hotel!"

The cover–ups. "The window with the mob view."

Uncovered. "Beat around that bush burning
for truth."

COINTELPRO Conspiracy. "Just hush up."

"Hush hell. Speak truth to power till power
tilts toward justice."

It's just us…
        We die.
        No, we live!

Emmett Till…
        We die
        No, we live!

Medgar Evers…
        We die
        No, we live!

Rosa Parks…
> She sat down
> No, she stood up!

Assata Shakur…
> She fled
> Yes, and she's free!

Fannie Lou Hamer…
> That little light of hers
> She let it shine!
> Let it shine
> Let it shine
> for us to envision
> to survive
> to strive
> to unite
> to organize
> to march
> in the millions
> and fight against all who
> seek to divide & destroy us.

FADE TO BLACK…

Heard 'Em Cry

We are an historical people
How can we not make history
Repeatedly
The slave narratives told by the griots
Echo from antiquity
Up into the 21st century
The invisibles given a visual
Enslaved inna strange land
Our story is biblical
Gruesome & beautiful
The ballot or the bullet crucible
That ultimatum still crucial
Mutual dreams deferred but never died
Another one finally realized
In 2008 on election night
Heard 'em cry: "YES WE CAN!"
And my afro felt justified
A legion of Black Martyrs
rose up
stirred up
The still waters creepin' thru my depths
Testified to the meaning in their deaths
Admonished me that it's still struggle left
With Brotha Obama
Be proud but expect mo' drama
Beware of the snake charmers
tighten ya armor
grow smarter
pray harder
reach farther
        for enlightenment whenever it gets darker
Come hell or high water!

Dystopia

Welcome to the year 3000
where the $tars descend upon earth & abort nature's rebirth
engulfed in artificial worth & pain that permeates opaque souls
still chocolate ghettos that despair clutches in a choke hold
&
vanilla suburbs melt down & erode
population control is handled by pandemic incarceration
manipulation of the global economy via premeditated inflation
ten of the most powerful corporations have closed ranks
to coerce in the Newest World Order
Illuminati mandates abolished all borders
soothsayers prophesy about satan's rule getting shorter
flying cars scud thru clouds over crowds of the thirsty masses
who intercept rain before it hits the sky
&
lick away tears before they get to cry
up high the silk–stockings live heavenly in space
thinking they're safe from the boom
their vacations are intergalactic time–sharing
on the periphery of the moon
for crude jokes they drop bread crumbs out of the sky
hoodwinking religionists into believing it's
manna from the Most High

manufactured hope to keep them pacified
with suspended memories of
the freedom fighters who fought & died
their torches abandoned with no fire
so the youth suffer
conditioned to fear the oppressor
they lash out at each other
welcome to time frozen — turning to rot
comprised of the few who have
& the most who have not...

FEEDBACK

A jaded generation. Faded cerebrals.
Mothership sightings. Psyched–out people.
Satellite oppression. Idiot–box fumes.
Toxic equinox. Hip Hop over the moon.
Commercial thugs, giddy up!
Mic check tunes.

1–2... 1–2.

From Zulus to jigaboos.
Mic checka. 1–2.
Armored ignorance in bulletproof.
Mic check tunes. 1–2... 1–2

Mic checka.
Mic checka.
1–2.
1–2.

Ring tone def. Left dumb, deaf & blind.
On ya mark. Get ready. It's rat race time!
Go, Negro, Go!
At 100 miles. Running backwards.
Feet of clay crackin'. 3rd eye cataracts.

Dysfunctional zodiac emcee. Nth degree cultural rape.
Monkey see. Monkey ape.
Guerrilla market mixtape: a little dis. Some self–hate.
Images copped off of Ebay.
Birthrights swapped for sordid mandrakes.
Swallow it down. Regurgitate. Savor the bitter aftertaste.
Then.
Go
Negro.
Go brush yo' grille.

Better

life doesn't always feel good
but it tends to feel better
once you've overcome

what you know 'bout love?

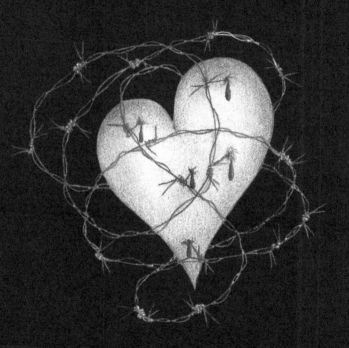

Despite the wilderness we're lost in
Somehow we found us

On Auto–Pilot

my heart takes flight with no wings
soaring thru sweet sounding smoke screens
blown from pipe dreams
what might love mean
to a man imbued with brittle heartstrings
traumatically ruled by a dread of being wooed
fooled & misused
feelings left battered
bruised & abandoned
understanding that unspoken words speak the most truth
so i creep between the lines to find proof
hoping i make it thru the maze unscathed
i gaze both ways for emotional scammers
instincts drenched in suspense on cliff hangers
as i sweep past danger
back to safety

Convicted

this Woman
whom they judge
suffers and forgives
in her stubborn conviction
she pleads for love
with a heart broken into infinite pieces
of scrap metal
&
withering olive branches

4bit10

U r the soulmate of my affection
a lotus flower afloat on still waters
running deep through my essence
effervescent
alluring
we bond poetically
a merged rhyme & rhythm
perfected thru our imperfections
we r perfect 4 each other
this reflected in the heartfelts we exchange
&
share in
sharing ourselves

at times i deny reality
in order 2 become 1 with U in fantasy
dreaming of milk & honey
despite the wilderness we're lost in
somehow we found us
&
discovered something 4bit10 2 eat
from the tree of life in this barren garden

i taste danger & find it delicious
the passion fruit of our labor 2 remain
hidden in plain sight
we steal away in stolen glimpses
our eyes conveying the unspeakable
as we consider surrender 2 the inevitable

my lips hunger 4 u
aching 2 kiss & caress away your every abuse
& loneliness
your every heartache & source of insecurity
'til your every sadness feels 4ever wonderful

Overblown

Underway

their genesis dates back untold calendars
distant lovers gather together for sharing
shrouded feelings hurting to be EXpressed

Overcautious

two hearts tiptoeing around each other
both innocent in aching for fulfillment
and guilty of sidestepping what fulfills

Undertones

fearful of emptying out their emptiness
they go as deep as words
profound ex–changes limit them to inaction

Overblown

articulate proverbs that parody breakups like:

love suppressed turns inwards against itself
then mutates into acid that eats gaping holes
into wholeness

proverbs pregnant in the poetic like:

love expressed speaks louder than wounds
and makes music that cures brokenness

Then Became Eve

smoldering doubts
gasped out prayers
my voice runs dry
tuneless in the twilight
crickets crowd my throat
heartbeats enhance
expanding my thorax
depression invades the vacancy
pressure rips open my ribs
bones dry & cracking
feeling torn
dashed hopes choke me
choked me 'til she spoke:
"You disentangled me, Black man.
my escape came thru you. I am
now free to be…"
her revelation intimates healing
the split in my rib cage becomes
the door to my heart
i reach out to her
to welcome her back
inside of us
we belong together

Drawn

in my probe for love
i slipped
i stumbled
i tripped into her stratosphere
humbled
star–struck & starry–eyed
by the star–power she possessed
magical how she finessed
my
heart
away
from
me
she split every atom in my anatomy
the fission conjured peace
gave me release

freed my nucleus
of
passion unknown
she set a blaze in my bones
the prospect of our separation
is the spillage of nuclear radiation
i am at home
&
safe in the expanse of her space
the gravity of her grace
quickens the force of attraction
keeping me gravitating
deeper
into
the
epicenter of our intimacy

SNAPSHOTS

PRESENT pre–TENSE

come closer
will yourself into my tempo of life
it can't be too out of tune
with yours
since everything else seems to be
dying around us
...MOTIONING

i am stranded
on one side of this door
you're listening from the other side
i strain to hear your soft–spoken attention
thru this glass partition
we fail to see "us"
in one another
too many words clutter our vision
...BLINDSIDED

PAST pre–TENSION
(cruising down memory lane)

i came along
alone
toting an arsenal of dried–up dreams
&
emotional luggage
she nudged me awake
unpacked my past
laundered it in the washbowl of her soul
hung it out to dry
under the sunshine inside her spirit
i haven't yawned since
....CLEANSED

she cracked the code
to my vault of faults
climbed inside
&

locked herself in for safekeeping
....DECIPHERED

she caressed open my wounds
dissected my pain
then spirited away the scabs
now without closure
how am i to heal?
.....DIS-EASED

BYGONES GOING
(colliding on memory lane)

she left
a love note
in my broken heart
&
expected me to read it
without bleeding
....STAINED

ICELAND

she froze our path
with her silence
i slipped
we slid
into a frostbitten schism
without enough fervor in our love
to thaw itself
......POLARized

she used her misery
to dig my grave
not knowing that i am deeper
than six feet
......MEMORIALIZED

GOING ON & ON

we have moments
when our lies
teach a deeper truth than
....NOTHING....AT ALL
......DISREGARD, PLEASE!

105

Release

she's air under the wings of my imagination
ventilation inside this suffocation
i caught a second wind for life thru her luv for life
&
sighed
release
exultant in peace
no matter how briefly she manages to free me
from what only she can fulfill—a gift
she unwraps & unpacks me
her impact beautifies my wounds
makes them bleed unbloody with purpose
this Sistah digs me deep
way deep beneath the surface
she's able to reinterpret my past pain & reapPRAISE its worth:
a garden divine
she unearths infinite acres of diamonds
clustered throughout my interior design
together we strike pay dirt

&
feel valued in the increase
as i decrease & prosper thru humility
it humbles me to pray to He Who's up there
for She who walks the earth a Servant Queen
crowned with faith that awakens the dream
emotions spring to my fingertips
whenever i write about this Mountain Woman
who is too heavy for etymology to carry
what she means to me
feelings that no prose amount could accommodate
luv that poetry could only insinuate
affection that inspires the heart to levitate
She's air under the wings of my imagination
ventilation inside this suffocation
i caught a second wind for life thru her luv
for me & sighed
release

Agency

will yourself to love you
no matter how others hate you

TIPSY

you got me tipsy
sippin' on memories of you
smiling beautifully
frowning righteously
speaking in elegant symphony
your melody pours thru my meditations
your rhythms surge my sensuality
your laughter is ear lavender
my cup runneth over
the love flows on
we are learning
to flow on in it

Roderick 'Rudy' Bankston   ~

What You Know 'Bout Love?
Jevon Jackson & Rudy ponder love

Jevon:
Someone once told me that Hate is the 2nd most deadliest
weapon of all. The Most Deadliest... Love. Romantic
Love. Mister–Missus Right Love. Sexin'–All–Night–Love.
For–Her–You'll–Sacrifice–our–Life–Love. The kinda Love
that seems impossible the first 20 years or so of your Life,
and then one night you wake up late, you look over at her
with her sleepy face and you're like "Damn, there I am!!"
You see You in her. And the reflection of yourself within
something so beautiful... it intoxicates you. And it's like
with every sip of her kiss you get more and more drunk
with adoration for her until you can't stagger any longer
and you fall face first deep into it... deep into Love.
That's why it's called "fall in love," you're so drunk with
it you can't help but to fall. And when you fall, what else
can you do but surrender to its fascinating energy.

Rudy:
Yeah, brah, i'm vibin' with ya theory, but see—me
I struggle with love. i recall days smiling inwardly
while thoughts of her tickled me. Til this very day, my
memory worships her warm walnut–brown eyes...they
epitomized sunshine beaming tender rays that held my
heart hostage—had me coming down with the Stockholm
Syndrome, captivated by her spunk, her touch, loving

the head–rush as her affections showered me like rapids.
The passion mimicked waterfalls, ours converging and
splurging on our love. i couldn't hold water as we sailed
up stream, amphibian lovers, afloat, landing ashore, only
to skyrocket to the moon where we made love and simul–
climaxed amongst the quasars...and fell 'cause i fell, i fell,
i fell in love.

Jevon:

But wait a minute—when you fell, did you land on solid
Earth? Or did you slip and fall on comets into the heart
of a broken universe? Cuz Love must be stable to last and
built on something real, like jumbo planes and freight
trains—weigh heavy with what you feel. And get deep
with what you feel, practice what you feel, don't be
scared with what you feel. Cuz I only know of two types
of armies tough enough to man a war—those who fashion
their physical weapons and the soldiers of love who brave
the field, with no armor, no ammo, no aim—just a Heart
and a Reason to smile for something wonderful.

Rudy:

Now understand, Brotherman, i did land on a solid rock
of hope—tossed inna sea of uncertainty—and hey, at
the time it worked for me. Never worried me how long
i could hold my breath trying to make it float. Maybe
this love could've swallowed all the water of the sea —
without drowning her or me. Imagine it, love caveats: keep

it steadfast and passionate. Reaching for the heart but
never grabbing it. Expressing how i felt with a 5 yr.
old's honesty—that feature exposed the man in me.
MACHISMO? Hell no! That paralyzes love—while open
emotions is like the Viagra of love—minus the artificial
stimulation—the courage to love is a natural nitrate in
love's orchard. Our union inspired the constellation to
spangle our love. We converted pain to rain and used it
to nourish our thang—it helped to maintain the beauty of
our love—locking our hearts into an unshakable, an
unbreakable hug. Homie, that's love.

Jevon:
Yeah, that Romantic Love is some courageous stuff. But
then you have this other Love that you can never get
enough. It's the sick kinda Love that turns platinum to rust
and diamonds to dust, it's the kinda Love that would make
a grown man leave his wife in the middle of the night—
The Love Of Money! A lust by design, it clones and copies
Love as it hugs and cuddles the mind, and all you can
think about is the shuffling sounds of the money machine
and the Ka–ching Ka–ching of the bank teller's endeavor
to count the cool crisp cash in a hurry—you grab your
stash and make slow sweet Love to it. Caressing two 50's
between your fingertips, thinkin' of all the kinky things
you could do with a 20 and a 10 and five sexy singles.
Money—you look into its soft green eyes knowing that
you'd do ANYTHING for it. You'd lie for it, blaze the sky

for it, get gun and vie for it, you'd even die for it—that's a sick, sick Love right there.

Rudy:

Oh, you talkin' 'bout that tangible green love—a broke man's dream love—but I done peeped the richest men who ain't seen Love.... Love Of Money? Without doubt or contradiction, I've witnessed this phenomenon growin' up—just to reminisce makes my mind throw up—vomit bitter memories that could rob the sweetest sugar daddy of all his saccharine—I'm tellin' ya man, I done watched the rust and the dust make a mockery of this love that's adorned with "In God We Trust"—crispy bills or dirty wrinkled dollars—hollers without speaking—a Pretty Young Tender that's legal and keeps the heart beating— down, down, down 'til it sees hell—thinking it's where the angels dwell—Love of Money? Can't tell me it's not the root of evil, the devil's puppet master—forecaster of disaster. This love of green paper cuts—will leave a man bleeding cesspools of greed... A filthy richness enables a crook to get away clean—after being seen. This love corrupts a person's moral integrity—peek-a-boo spooky Love that frightens the hell outta me.

Bars That Hold

These bars that hold me
awarded us acquaintance
i acknowledge your tailormade station
in my life

These bars that hold me
situated us 2 go Dutch & share heartfelt sentiments
no subject is contraband
since our eyes learned to schmooze

These bars that hold me
could never clog our chemistry
its symmetry defies the inelegant elements
inside this confinement

These bars that hold me
will never tune out your redemptive soprano
your serenade is salvation
you save me from the cacophony

These bars that hold me
obliged me 2 treasure the exquisite texture
of your womanhood

It blankets me inside this icebox
thank you 4 keepin' me thawed

These bars that hold me
softened my stance against exploring uncharted territory
our footprints baptize the trajectory we are on
unsure of the destination but committed 2 goin' 2gether

These bars that hold me
freed us 2 gaze
2 imagine
2 build beyond these bars that hold me

A 21 Word Love Story

Insightful
Seeing her essence opened his eyes

Attached
Becoming one, they grew young together

Epilogue
They laughed, they cried, they lasted

Let It Burn

Kindled
old flames hidden in plain sight

Steamy
passions smolder under the ash heap

Hot Air
their smoke signals spell out misunderstanding

Ex-tinguished
They move closer and closer apart

Firetrap
Love that once enlivened them now consumes them

Yours & Mine

A smile that radiates
Keeps the heart glowin'
Genuine words that penetrate
While keepin' the mind growin'

A love that's committed
In times of rain or shine
All that nourishes is permitted
To enter the realm of yours & mine

Can romance be real
One of love's contradictions
It's about what we feel
That gives a clear definition

A solid foundation
Keeps us down to earth
A sincere dedication
Helps build up the worth

Determined — we'll make it
So let's journey on to destiny
Fate comes clothed & naked
During states of agony & ecstasy

gathering the pieces

It dawned on me
in the wee hours of falling down to
rock bottom
that I was born on the shoulders of giants

Roderick 'Rudy' Bankston ～

This chapter contains poems written since my return to life above ground. Their creation is balm for the slow, painful, and necessary process of my healing.

These poems will appear in a collection of post–prison poetry to be published in 2019.

A Lonely Place

healing is a lonely place
i live there
each day claiming space to
feel inside my wounds for medicine
the scabs must be sick of me by now
my propensity is to pick on them
&
pick at them
until they lose credibility
they are too unconvincing
to give cover to the source of my superpowers

Echoes of You

Redolence

the fragrance from the secret tears you shed
has weeped into my soul
looming like cologne called *she breathe*s
so all the more you breathe through me
& dream through insomnia

Ownership

you possess my heart
but i wish i could hand it to you
devoid of the heaviness you feel
and the heaviness i feel over how you feel

Delineation

the boundaries between delight and sorrow
are marked by our separation
we stand on the same side of promise
your peace marks the beginning of piece of mind for me
i wage luv over you

Ghosts

those phantoms causing you to doubt are just that:
phantoms
make–believe assumptions given undeserved power

Sister Comrade

your power is made omnipotent from spirit
stand & speak & walk proudly & unafraid in it
for it is grace that has brought you this far
not man
nor flesh
nor what lies right underneath
but Who towers deepest within & highest above

Love

the beautiful thing is that we are
just what we are
stronger than our weaknesses
bolder than our fears
and authentic in our bond

if you ever hear anyone ask about me and love
and who loved me into the most authentic me
you clear your throat & stare the questioner
dead in the eye
like you're the only answer because you are
the only reflection of it

The North Star

it dawned on me
in the wee hours of falling down
to rock bottom
that i was born on the shoulders of giants
who stood taller than Kilimanjaro
played frisbee with the moon
& sculpted maps to freedom
in the constellations

Residuals

she asked me to write her a love poem
to create fiction out of the hurt
she sweet talked me into accepting
maybe it was my ego that convinced me
that my love was potent enough
to transform the cinderblock in her chest
into a flowerbed
by the time i could smell the roses
i had pruned my nose to mask my face
now i breathe through my wounds
to keep from smothering myself

Tragicomedy

Darkness overshadows us from within
The sequel to what we've experienced from without
A chemical reaction
Nothing happens in a vacuum
i wish i would've known to take a knee
upon first hearing their national anthem
Lyrics that praise our oppression
We were never taught to sing for ourselves
or that we even had a voice
nor the choice to reject making heroes out of our hitlers
The founding fathers don't deserve statues either
abraham lincoln neither
since he really didn't want to free us
Break the ground to memorialize John Brown
i mean, Mike Brown
That would be amazing grace with the sweet sound
Lace the American landscape
with sculptures of every victim shot down
With their hands up to remind us
that life ain't been no crystal stair for colored folk
But we still willed ourselves to elevate
in the most dire straits we were compelled to levitate
for Heaven's sake

Faith and tenacity that defied gravity —
We've choked out laughs to keep from crying inside this
tragicomedy
Although some tears are swallowed to ward off thirst
for droughts that grow worse in this land of
opportunity gaps

Animal Instincts

oppression is a chameleon
altering its form to keep us uninformed
a lizard blending into political correctness
it is never just black and white
any gray area is a mirage
the colorblind lens is dogmatism
on the leash of ignis fatuus
that depth of ignorance is fatuous
whose privilege is it to let this sleeping dog lie in wait
for us to dig our own graves
we were never slaves
we were enslaved

No Revisions

my past pain glows in the darkness
&
flashes light out of the sunken place
i refuse to descend beneath me
cast your spells in another direction
i've slain too many witch doctors to drink from that brew
the true self knows what it knows
to play ignorant to my history is to ignore my story
&
act out a script with too many revisions
you can't narrate a truth you've never lived
&
barely understand
a man's wounds are his teachers
they hold a healing curriculum
avoidance is too steep a price to pay
living in denial eventually leads to psychosis
the God in me can not suffer atheism
false prophecies profit no one in the long run
the legs eventually give out
what would it profit either of us to lose
in a game no longer worth competing in
i won't go blind to see something that is not there

Spoken

ofttimes
i must speak the unspoken
when the passion gets too intense to withhold
without drowning myself from within
words save me from imploding
the fuse was lit
when i first realized who you were
&
that i was supposed to love you
going against everything i thought i believed in
love does that when it deepens into rare form
it disrupts who we thought we were
what we thought we knew & stood for
our love obsoletes standing
we took flight
on wings that fluttered with a butterfly effect

Compromised

they appraised us 3/5 human
heathen flesh
animal penis
monetized womb
the rest — God body
to be feared without reverence
&
whipped Into what their demons
could bow to & worship as inferiors
to mirror their hidden complex

Dear Mirror

i demand that you not delude me
into distorted views of myself
reveal when it is clearly me
so that i know to stand down
&
check my ego in those situations
also reflect lucidly when it is them
so that i know to stand up
&
assert my respect in all situations
offer me no blind spots
expose me

Also by Roderick "Rudy" Bankston:

Snippets of Soul in Seventeen Syllables

This slim volume contains haiku written in prison and in freedom. Its contents cover topics of history, love, culture, and life distilled into the ancient poetry form of haiku.

ISBN-13:978-1547170524

Shed So Many Tears

A novel of shared struggle, soul-searching, and discovery. Liz is a mother on a mission, dedicated to single–parenting her only child, Malik, into manhood while helping him avoid his imprisoned father's plight...or something worse: the pitfalls of the Milwaukee streets.

ISBN 0-7414-6725-9

Order copies at iAmWeClassics.com

Learn more about Rudy and his work at

iAmWeClassics.com

"One writes out of one thing only — one's own experience. Everything depends on how relentlessly one forces from this experience the last drop, sweet or bitter, it can possibly give."   ~ James Baldwin